j811.54 N994c
Cast away :poems for our
time /
Nye, Naomi Shihab,

MAY 0 8 2020

D0312643

Cast
Away
Poems
for Our
Time

NAOMI SHIHAB NYE

Cast Away

Poems for Our Time

GREENWILLOW BOOKS

An Imprint of HarperCollinsPublishers

Cast Away: Poems for Our Time
Copyright © 2020 by Naomi Shihab Nye

All rights reserved. No part of this book may be used or
reproduced in any manner whatsoever without written permission
except in the case of brief quotations embodied in critical articles
and reviews. Printed in the United States of America.
For information address HarperCollins Children's Books,
a division of HarperCollins Publishers,
195 Broadway, New York, NY 10007.
www.epicreads.com

The text of this book is set in 11-point Geometric 415 BT.
Book design by Paul Zakris

Library of Congress Cataloging-in-Publication Data

Names: Nye, Naomi Shihab, author.
Title: Cast away : poems for our time / by Naomi Shihab Nye.
Description: First edition. | New York : Greenwillow Books, 2019. |
Includes indexes. |
Summary: "Poet Naomi Shihab Nye shines a spotlight
on the things we cast away, from plastic water bottles to refugees"
—Provided by publisher.
Identifiers: LCCN 2019021149 | ISBN 9780062907691 (hardback)
Subjects: LCSH: Children's poetry, American.
Classification: LCC PS3564.Y44 C37 2019 | DDC 811/.54—dc23
LC record available at https://lccn.loc.gov/2019021149

19 20 21 22 23 PC/LSCH 10 9 8 7 6 5 4 3 2 1
First Edition

Greenwillow Books

For Cathy Song

I couldn't save the world,
but I could pick up trash.

Honolulu

Blue plastic ring

no setting

no stone

found on Diamond Head Road

Contents

ROUTE 1: Sweepings

ROUTE 2: Titters & Tatters

ROUTE 3: Odds & Ends

ROUTE 4: Willy-nilly

ROUTE 5: Residue

Taking Out the Trash

by Kamilah Aisha Moon

Someone else used to do this before.
Someone responsible,
someone who loved me enough
to protect me from my own filth
piling up.

But I'm over 40 now & live alone,
& if I don't remember it's Thursday
& rise with the cardinals & bluejays
calling up the sun, I'm stuck
with what's left rotting
for another week.

I swing my legs like anchors over the side
of the bed & use the wall for leverage
to stand, shuffle to the bathroom.
In summer, I slide into a pair of shorts & flip flops,
wandering room to room to collect
what no longer serves me.

I shimmy the large kitchen bag from
the steel canister, careful not to spill
what's inside or rip it somehow
& gross myself out.
Sometimes I double bag for insurance,
tying loose ends together,
cinching it tightly for the journey.

Still combing through webs of dreams,
of spiders' handiwork glistening above
the wheeled container on the back patio,
I drag my refuse down the driveway
past the chrysanthemums & azaleas,
the huge Magnolia tree shading the living room
from Georgia's heat, flattening hordes
of unsuspecting ants in my path to park it
next to the mailbox for merciful elves
to take off my hands.

It is not lost on me that one day

someone responsible,

someone who loves me enough

will dispose of this worn, wrinkled

container after my spirit soars on.

I don't wait to say thank you

to those doing this grueling, necessary work.

But I do stand in the young, faintly lit air

for a long moment to inhale deeply,

& like clockwork when he strides by,

watch the jogger's strong, wet back

fade over the slight rise of the road.

(Copyright © 2018 by Kamilah Aisha Moon. Originally published in Poem-a-Day on October 24, 2018, by the Academy of American Poets)

Cast
Away
Poems
for Our
Time

Introduction

How much have you thrown away in your lifetime already? Do you ever think about it?

I'd like to see the things I threw away when I was eight or twelve or fourteen.

The words *discard* or *refuse* don't seem appealing. *Rubbish*—often associated with the UK—is a cozy word, like baby rabbits living inside tree stumps.

Whatever you call it, trash and litter—its existence on planet Earth—has fascinated me for a long time. There are places you can't get away from it—the aftermath of a Fiesta parade in my city of San Antonio, for example—or the back streets of Mumbai, which many people still prefer to call Bombay. I heard there wasn't any trash in Japan. So of course it was something I looked for right away upon arrival there and felt weirdly joyous to find a two-inch-tall yellow pencil on a beach, which instantly became the King of Pencils in my cloth pencil pouch.

Trash cans used to be quirkier. Some were short, others metal, plastic, some green, some a debonair shiny silver, some with handles or separate lids . . . but now many Americans are living in the era of institutional giant cans, with wheels and handles. They seemed like scary animals at first. You can easily sprain your wrist dragging a heavy one by one hand only, but this is all so they can be picked up by the two massive robotic arms of the trash truck, which is actually very fun to watch, if you are two years old. Clamp, lift, dump—it's a hug at every house—an urban rhythm.

Cheers to the cities and stores that are banning plastic bags. Long overdue! Obviously it's possible to use the same paper or cloth bag for a very long time, if you just train yourself to carry it in. And isn't it totally time to say farewell to straws that pierce and torture fish? We're all involved in this. The animals that die from eating plastic bags deserve better protection from humans. This is my very obvious advice to people who want to make less trash. Reusable implements. Buy food items with less packaging if possible. Decline the extra napkins and utensils if you don't really need them. Carry your own cup. It's just a matter of getting into different habits.

Kids probably know more about the five trillion pieces of plastic in the oceans, in great swirling garbage patches, than many adults do. The largest scary congregation—Great Pacific Garbage Patch—lives somewhere in that beautiful blue water between Hawai'i and California. Good luck to the various styles of giant trash vacuums—the Seabin Project, for one—headed out into the waters from different shores to consume all this junk. I hope you are very hungry, vacuums.

Where does this plethora of leavings come from? How long does it take you, even one little you, to fill the can by your desk?

I am assuming things—that you have a desk. Really, a desk is a great luxury on planet Earth. I am assuming you don't just throw everything onto the floor or ground around you when you are done with it. Apparently a lot of people still do that: see poems.

If you live in a remote rural place in any country, you may be more aware of how much you dispose of than someone who lives in a city—in a city, it's constantly being carted away. And it's shocking. It's shocking how much trash we make. What does that say about us?

I'm not sure why, but it always seemed like my job to pick up trash whenever I saw it. Perhaps this stems from being bicultural, belonging nowhere and everywhere at once, being a "pleaser," always trying to make my parents and friends happy, or perhaps it's a result of my preference for clean spaces.

Once I signed a piece of paper supposedly mailed by the City of San Antonio, promising to pick up all the trash in a four-to-six-block radius of our house for the rest of my life. Was there really such a document? I am sure of it, but I have never met another person who signed one. I know I contemplated it briefly, then signed with a flourish and sent the self-addressed stamped envelope back to our city refuse department, feeling proud. How did they know me so well?

Perhaps, though, my need to pick up trash stems from the fact that my mom was named the sloppiest person in her Soldan High School class senior yearbook (the same high school that Tennessee Williams attended years before her in St. Louis). School yearbooks used to declare such things—

Most Likely to Succeed, Best Dressed, Sloppiest. My mom, a highly intelligent person who skipped two grades and went to college at sixteen on a full scholarship, could eat crackers in her bed and leave the crumbs lying around for weeks, on the floor, even under her pillow. She could leave stacks of dirty plates in her room and be able to fall asleep anyway.

Even now (she's a chipper ninety-one), she prefers to pile up catalogs, hoards junk mail, retains snack bags, and never hangs up clothes. Why should she? She could wear the same ones tomorrow! Old newspapers rise in towers by every chair. But she can still do the entire crossword puzzle in fifteen minutes and is very particular and accurate about many things. She reads five books at once and is a treasure trove of random details. Once my brother and I threw out some of her kitchen spices that were forty years old. These are not habits she has tried to cure, nor is she a bit ashamed of them. So naturally, as her daughter and older child attempting to maneuver through life, I was born the cleanup crew.

And sometimes there were payoffs to being a trash collection girl. One happy day, age ten, I went out by myself in Ferguson, Missouri, with one dime in my pocket to buy a delicious orange-and-white Creamsicle on a stick at a corner store, and there, glittering by the mailbox, lay one shiny quarter. Sweet treat and bounty, at once! Feeling unexpectedly rich, I kept it for a long time.

Another happy day was finding a muddy yellow glove I had accidentally dropped into the stream months earlier. It was hard to recognize, draped on a twig.

Trash bags, silver tongs, and cotton garden gloves stay close at hand for my duties. I don't have superlong tongs like professional people who clean parking lots, with click-and-pinch devices so you don't have to stoop. The bending is part of the rhythm to me. It's trash yoga.

Recently I was happy to learn of a Swedish trend called plogging, founded by Erik Ahlström, who moved from a rural location to Stockholm and was stunned by the amount of visible trash. So he encouraged people to jog and collect trash at the same time. He made it popular! Plogging has recently been booming and spreading to other countries, including the USA.

You might also look up a documentary film called *Trash Dance*, made by Allison Orr and Andrew Garrison in Austin, Texas, which shines a new light on collection vehicles, demonstrating that even they can dance.

> *Beauty in the lumbering roll of giant machines*
> *crisscrossing in dark parking lot   intersecting*
> *spinning   turning*
> *We live in such a trashy time*
> *trashy chatter   trashy clutter*
> *How to love what we are given remains the task*
> *How to transform or enhance*
> *what we have*

In Berlin, Germany, I once stayed in a beautiful hotel called Bleibtreu ("Stay true") for six weeks. On one of my last mornings there, I picked up trash in a pocket park

I'd been walking through every day, because by then it was my problem as much as anyone else's. In Germany I wasn't sure what all the rustling wrappers came from— long, lovely, vowel-laden German names printed on them—sausages, crackly candies? Junk, junk, junk. Old men sat on green park benches, gripping leashes of small dogs, staring at me, but not unkindly.

In San Antonio, where I have lived most of my life, we now have a regular one-day Basura Bash where dozens of people wearing yellow T-shirts pick up trash from our beautiful riverbanks. Cans, wrappers, clogging Styrofoam cups . . . each person with a sack, wearing gloves . . . like a club, a party. It is mind-boggling how much trash collects around a river. Maybe this group could start our local plogging chapter this year.

Is trash one of our biggest problems on our lovely shared Earth? Is it one of our many biggest problems; does it connect to a lot of other problems? If tiny plastic particulates are being found in the fish that people eat, then entering the tummies of humans . . . not hard to see a chain of events unfolding.

I feel a bit anxious any time I'm out and about without my gear and see something that needs to be picked up. My fingers feel itchy. That's my job.

Some people focus on other people's trash. A man named Paul Moran ransacked trash bins in front of the writer John Updike's home for years. You can see some of his collection on a blog called *The Other John Updike Archive*.

This activity has certain invasive, stalker-esque qualities, but if you read about Paul Moran, it seems he conducted his hobby with respectful fascination. He loves "relics" and "assemblage art pieces." There are also peculiar YouTube videos of people around the country collecting treasures— desks, lamps, record cabinets, frying pans—from other people's curbs on trash pickup day, even in the snow. I can imagine doing it, but I can't imagine filming it. Actually, it's a great way to furnish your rooms for little money. My favorite tiny chest-of-drawers, in which I keep stationery and envelopes, was found on a discarded heap of furniture on Mulberry Street. I painted it yellow, added little green glass drawer handles, and voilà! A treasure.

Once I stayed in a hotel in Toronto where an early handwritten draft of the famous John Lennon song "Imagine" is smoothed out and displayed in a glass case in the lobby. I think John was working on it in his room and threw that draft away.

Anyone can stay awake worrying about where everything ultimately goes. Into loaded secret landfills? And what about the population explosion that no one likes to mention, and the travesty of disposable diapers, how long it takes anything to decompose and how many things never will?

On Deer Isle, Maine, there's an open-to-the-public landfill—the official paid trash staff lines up the best bounty recently collected on shelves in a tiny house. Free! Chipped ancient plates, latches, screens, green rags, doll heads, vintage picture books . . . one could go from being a trash collector to becoming a hoarder very quickly.

David Sedaris, one of everyone's favorite writers, has always picked up trash, too. He writes about it in some of his books, especially *Theft by Finding*, and has recently had a trash truck named after him—PIG PEN SEDARIS—in Horsham district, West Sussex, England. Though I have no similar ambition, I think of him when out walking to our own little lovely grocery store three blocks from our house, fishing bus tickets and receipts and wrappers out of the grasses. Many times I am overwhelmed, just in three blocks, as the bag gets quickly full. As Sedaris has written, "On foot, nothing escapes my attention: a potato-chip bag stuffed into the hollow of a tree, an elderly mitten caught in the embrace of a blackberry bush, a mud-coated matchbook at the bottom of a ditch."

Sometimes we have to leave things. You never know what's out there. Selection is involved.

Naomi Shihab Nye
San Antonio, Texas

ROUTE 1
Sweepings

Little Red Purse, London

Outside Ottolenghi, a restaurant popular

for bringing Arab and Jewish cuisines together,

a woman picking through a giant rubbish bin

warbled as I walked by—"You! You, come here!"

She handed me a small woven bag,

Tibetan maybe, red and brown striped,

three fluffy pompoms stitched to each side.

The purse seemed fresh, wrapped in white tissue.

"This looks more like you than me," she proclaimed.

What?

"That hippie look—more like you."

I was dressed nicely,

hair brushed, neat black skirt,

and she called me that?

This was three years ago.

Ever since, it's been my favorite purse.

Two

Two white buttons
not matching
in hot white gravel
dreaming of
shirts

Trash Talk

Let's just throw it away.
We can get a new one.

Why recycle?
Someone's just making money off it.

You know that company that says
their shoes are made out of soda bottles?
Yeah right, my head is made out of peanuts.

Sorrow of the Paper Mill

"Every question was like the snapping of a little thread about my heart."
—Dorothy Wordsworth

Birds knew the branches of these great straight trunks,

piled high upon one another in the trucks

    of Duluth, Minnesota.

Birds made simple knitted nests, circling, resting

    in foliage

of deep green, knew how to live unseen from

    the predatory eyes

of owl and eagle, remembered how to hide.

    Where did my home go?

Once a child told us a forest is really a room.

    Chop it chop it chop it!

Why why why? Every little question

    answered by money.

Flatbeds and factories, making

shiny newspaper inserts advertising what

few people seem to want or need.

How many of us throw them away

before we look at a newspaper?

    How many glossy scraps?

O magnificent giant trees, your lives were in vain.

World of the future, we thirsted

Stripped of a sense of well-being,
we downed our water from small disposable bottles.
Casting the plastic to streetside,
we poured high-potency energy tonics or Coke
down our throats, because this time in history
had sapped us so thoroughly and
we were desperate.
Straws, plastic caps, crushed cans,
in a three-block walk you could fill a sack.

As if we could replenish spirits quickly,
pitching containers without remorse—
who did we imagine would pick them up?
What did we really know of plastic spirals in the sea
bigger than whole countries,
we had never swirled in one ourselves,

as a fish might do, a sea urchin, a whole family of eels,

did we wish to be invincible, using what we wanted,

discarding what we didn't, as in wars,

whole cities and nations crumpled

after our tanks and big guns pull out?

How long does it take to be thirsty again?

We were so lonely in the streets though

all the small houses still had noses, mouths,

eyes from which we might peer, as our fellow-

citizens walk their dogs, pause helplessly as the dogs

circle trees, tip their heads back for a long slow slug

of water or tea, and never fear, never fear.

"DON'T MESS WITH TEXAS" (highway sign)

Really?

What about these energy bottles pitched by someone

who didn't have energy   to find a bin?

Fun Finger Food wrappers dropped by someone

not so fun?

Empty envelopes scattered outside post office

Pepper packets

from a sad lunch where two people broke up

Shortbread cookie wrapper

missing the Highlands of Scotland

(*This is not my real home*)

plastic bags windswept   forlorn   torn

STRIKE WHILE IT'S HOT says the lottery ticket

but it's always hot these days

"Don't mess with Texas" was said to be

the anti-litter campaign that really worked?

but not here—on old streets called

Guadalupe and Camp

turtles paddling San Pedro Creek

swimming wide around pitched green bottles

not sure what they are

diving deep when you wave

HEY!

Only a few days ago two human beings

toasted one's birthday by clinking those bottles

and now they're stuck on rocks

Random Trash Thoughts

You don't find much that's pink.

Blocks around elementary schools
are surprisingly free of litter.
Good custodians?
Kids are better than grown-ups?

Outside Bonham Elementary, one small white scrap
with *Party Games* handwritten on it.
        Trash Treasure Hunt might qualify.

You don't find many toys.

And what of the mind? The drifting little thoughts
    that never find a place to land?

Once at Kailua Beach on O'ahu
half buried in soft sand
we uncovered a perfect yellow bucket and shovel
that stayed with us ten years.

Walk the other side of street—
find different-style trash.
Sushi boxes, green Blistex tube.

Look at Me, Look at Me

Old political signs

fade outside voting centers

till they bend over at the waist,

let loose from their legs.

A man who ran for mayor

last time around

drifts into your front yard.

End of August

Someone went crazy with toilet paper.

Stalked South Flores Street wrapping it around

telephone poles.

Weaving the snag of old roots by the bus bench

now white, now tangled, in honor

of all that is unclean or heartbreaking or

not what we dream.

Take that, world.

Leavings

1

People were never trash.
Under the highway bridge,
in a bombed city, encamped under tarps,
people were still sons, teachers,
teenagers who wanted better clothes,
saxophonists, hairdressers, fruit vendors,
bus drivers, DJs, good dancers, grandmas,
nurses, photographers, computer experts,
maintenance technicians, managers,
shoe salesmen, excellent science students,
and something had gone wrong along the way.
Maybe it was not their fault or maybe
there were steps they could take toward improvement
but people were never trash, just as
leaves were never litter.
Roots of a tree go deep. Under the sidewalk,
below the ancient foundation,
patient beyond measure.
What they have to survive.
Leaves piling on sidewalks after months of drought
deserve to be there as much as we do.

2

Long ago my friend David said,

More depends on good timing

than on anything else

and even though we were young

I knew he was right.

If that single telephone number

had stayed safe in your pocket

instead of blowing away from your lap . . .

a whole different life?

3

A preacher asked, Can you imagine
having to push every single thing you own
everywhere you go, on wheels?
Try putting all your troubles in a grocery cart,
and taking them with you every day.

That is what homeless means.
Troubles and treasures, all in one cart.
A weary woman had appeared at his front door
with her mounded burdens
asking if she could park for a while.

Camps of refugees exist all over the world
where one clean space to sleep
away from filth and stench
might feel like a miracle.

4

A boy took the bits of trash
he found on a walk,
and dumped them in the yard,
arranging them as one person's story.
First the man lost his sandpaper.
His baby was sucking on a blue pacifier
which is kind of like a baby's cigarette
but the baby lost it when they crossed the street
and cried very hard.
The mom was eating a fried cherry pie.
The little girl lost her spelling homework
with dust and trust on it
and here it is, see? Too bad,
she was a good speller.
They all dropped their bus transfers
in a big wind and read this torn-up newspaper
to find out what to do next.

5

We have no idea.

Hill Country

Deer drifting into yards at sundown for corncobs,
soggy watermelon rinds pitched onto compost—
Feed me, revive this dry evening,
rotten apple, soft banana, core of the pineapple . . .
seven deer stepping hopefully,
one tiny fawn learning the circuit.

Trash Is a Ticket to Nowhere

It says, I do not care
about you, pouf!
You can pick me up
if you want to,
the person who dropped me was
more important
than the person who picks me up.
What?

Make our smallest moves the right ones.
On a San Antonio street called Dallas,
the corner of Baltimore,
all of us connected, like it or not,
if we're alive, isn't it all ours?
Even the street called *Cary Grant?*
Bent wire, Styrofoam,
snaps. Here's the rim of a pizza box
from the Mesozoic era.
Trash says *disregard, disregard.*

Georgia O'Keeffe on Location

1

The housekeeper Margaret who worked
for the painter Georgia O'Keeffe
and her photographer partner Alfred Stieglitz
plucked streaky photographs
from his bin.
She pawed through Georgia's own trash
liking what she saw:
discarded sketches, false starts,
luminous studies in blue.
Consider it rescue.
Margaret kept these treasures in the attic
of the old family home at Lake George.
A long time later, her son got hold of the trove
and organized an art show, pinning up
half-baked drawings and stained photographs
by the corners, like children's artwork over a bed.
Wasn't it so interesting to see?
In some ways, more interesting than
anything final or complete?

Margaret's son could remember
Georgia slapping him across the cheek
when he was small—clearer
in memory than the days they got along.

2

At Ghost Ranch in New Mexico's desert,
Georgia O'Keeffe built her own home
atop an ancient rattlesnake nest.
Not knowing, not knowing.
Forever, while painting large calm canvases in her
    open garage,
Georgia would be beating insulted snakes off with
    her cane.

Find Your Path

Combed empty gravel

Nothing to be picked up

No one to be served

open acre of day

door to quiet

swings on its hinge

treasure trove

path of cool attention

What's here?

What's everywhere?

Do this daily

Even ten minutes

gathering corners of solitude

breeze

nothing else

not even thought

aids your sanity

Pine Cones

In a California redwood forest
breath feels bigger than all people
a note older than our ancestors
memories stirred by rustling
we will survive
hold a little beauty during difficult times
Quiet feels round as a planet
surely a bigger quiet
holds us all
Here is the queen of the pine cones
standing right against her own tree
full pride
It's fine not to know how to solve everything
It's still a room to sit in

Snow Covers All the Trash

Such muffling
of our human doings
See how little we are?

Everyone goes home
Good night, Portland, Oregon, at 3 p.m.
We'll eat whatever we have

Little potatoes soaked in salt
Talk to the person right next to us
Someone drives me in a tall truck with big wheels

Pristine white tracks down fresh streets
No cans no wrappers no leavings of humankind
Surprise!

Trash Talk 929

A friend says, "I'm so tired of men taking the credit."

Shortly after, I'm sitting with my mom on a

    wide hotel porch

under circulating fans when history floats in.

The woman who lived in this mansion 100 years ago

planted the first azaleas in Austin. Her fingers loosened

dry soil they preferred around their roots,

she learned what made them happy,

trimmed the wilted blossoms neatly.

Her glorious hedge grew great.

Just think, these were the *only azaleas* in town.

A real conversation piece. Azaleas stand out.

People came by in carriages and Model T's to see

the billowing pink and red flowers, so quickly a landmark.

She told everyone it was her husband's garden.

Who Do You Think You Are?

Cigarette butt cradled in billowing grass
by front gate—who stands here smoking
in the dark? Did some guy pitch it from his car
after the night shift heading home?

When I was a new driver, the passenger
in the car next to me at a very long stoplight
pitched a can out her open window
so hard it hit my door.
Stoplight still red, I jumped forth,
hurled it through her window.
Soda droplets flew. "You lost something?"
She looked stunned. Green light.
I jumped back into my car and zoomed.

Separated

Band-Aid printed with green turtles
crumpled by the road
at Ingleside on the Bay, Texas
I think I know
which little boy lost that
He'll fret when he sees it is missing

A few hundred miles from here
thousands of traumatized kids
huddle in cages
abandoned WalMarts
missing their *mamas y papas*
Who can believe this?
Land of the Free!
What can we know
of their stories, tears,
the fear their parents carried,
what you might have to drop
if you were walking across Mexico
or the actual moment
someone big seized the child
and told the parents to go?

How big was the wailing?
I cannot believe
what people do.

Later, could the border patrol agent
sleep easily?
His own kids in the bedroom next to his?
When I was seven, I read "The Hangman at Home"
by Carl Sandburg.
"Anything is easy for a hangman, I guess."
I had to ask, "What is a hangman?"
No one would tell me.

Our favorite Republican pal writes a note saying,
"At least the kids will be having regular meals
and recreational activities now,"
but I want to lie down
and cover my head with a pillow
as my father did
the day his own family
became refugees
so long ago.

Trash Talk 212

It may seem cruel, but surely for the greater good.

We must teach them a lesson.

Laws are righteous,

Laws must be followed.

Turn the other cheek.

Avert the gaze.

Never mind that our grandfathers, uncles, mothers,

crossed borders too.

They were trembling god-fearers,

pale-skinned brides of the future republic,

don't try to mix and match these days with those.

Our people were running from religious persecution,

drugs and gangs had nothing to do with their migrations,

it was all the word of This Lord or That Lord,

which makes our stories entirely different,

you have no idea what these people believe.

Found

One black button
in a small plastic bag
You suit my mood
Where would we begin
to stitch our country back together?
Who will make the buttonhole?
Z for zipper but who among us
could really craft one?

A single silver star
on a curb by Bonham Elementary
Good work!
Glimmering
like a treasure
stronger at this moment than all 50
drooping on the flagpole

Anger

It must have lived in the back pocket
of those jeans with the frayed cuffs you didn't wear
for more than a year
then suddenly flared

how sometimes
you can twist your back
by the smallest bend or
sitting strangely in a chair.
Drop it drop it drop it.
Stand up, stretch

into the can
into the drain
It cannot serve you now

ROUTE 2
Titters & Tatters

Little Boy and Green Trash Truck

He wads Kleenex into balls
plucks a knot of cat fur from carpet
a penny
stuffs it into his truck's open back door
then roars *Rum! Rum! Rum!*
crawling along the floor
power and joy and pride
as the real trucks
rumble through the streets
swinging around corners
outside

Tinfoil Merges with Street

pretends it could melt

sticks to pavement like ugly news

sticks to brain

Ads fade overnight

Half-priced ice cream

O swiftly disappearing sunset

Smashed cup

Whole world feels

bottoms up

Refugee zones

have trouble with trash

one of many services not offered

Dear August A. Busch

You wanted to sleep in a windmill
so you built one in south St. Louis
halfway between your house and your farm
a hundred years ago
there weren't any other windmills around
Son of two brewery magnates
you kept a cozy apartment under the blades
so you could eat and drink in comfort
when it was hard to get home
you'd curl up on snowy nights
giant horses tied in a stable outside
I think I love you   anyone kooky enough
to build a windmill
I'm sorry you suffered so much illness
and such a rough end
By now your treasured landmark
has been many restaurants
I don't see how anyone could pass Das Bevo mill
and not wish to eat there
white bowls of red cabbage   pickle-sweet dream
crispy fish   potato pancakes   applesauce
I almost don't want to tell you that today out walking

in San Antonio I found a crushed Busch beer can

in a hedge of white roses

and felt someone had trampled your name

What takes more energy

to stomp a can

or carry it to a proper resting place?

I want a windmill

painted yellow

even a very little one for the cat to sleep in

with a spinning propeller on its roof

singing singing singing

dreams can come true

At the Bus Stop

Titters & tatters
ripped bag tops
faded receipts
outdated transfers
tucked among
blossoming lantana tendrils—

What we make,
what the earth makes.
You need a whole new collection bag
for bus stops,
people spend a lot of messy time
on these benches.

I envy Canadians,
their ability to avoid us
when they want to,
hold on, North Star!
How gloomy we Americans are
these days,
lost in conflict,
lonesome for pride,
hunched up beside sacks
that once held chips.

Maui

A man walking a pig on a leash
asks if I would like to feed her. Uh, sure.
I kneel, he pours Cheerios into my hand,
Lilikoi has a wet snout and soft lips.
She's a very friendly pig, nuzzling gently,
gazing up at me for more.
He says, *Lilikoi is mellow.*
I can tell.
She's not trashy or messy at all.
Great.
Many people think pigs are dirty but look
how clean she is.
Perfect.

Red Ribbon on the Walk

After the bulldozers,
graders, noisy asphalt mixers,
lumber away for the tenth time,
trying to repave Sheridan Street,
poor old Sheridan
keeps cracking again
the minute it's new
due to the weight of buses
and ancient irrigation ditches
supposedly running beneath it,
I find you, long satiny red ribbon,
lying in the street.
Bulldozers dropping a red satin ribbon?
Seems unlikely.
Construction workers in helmets, orange vests . . .
leave a red ribbon?
Like the world we're in now.
Things that don't go together
confounding at every turn.
Sometimes we just have to close our eyes.
Think of something better.

Graceful egrets alighting

at exactly 8:26 p.m.

in their cypress tree

by the river

a block away.

Swooping in, perfectly timed,

coasting from all directions. In a world where people

are fighting, fighting, fighting.

Egrets, thank you.

Red ribbon,

are you a glimmer of hope?

Failure

On Valentine's Day
a single page of lined notebook paper
flutters loose in the park
I LOVE YOU
crossed out
I LOVE I
crossed out (and who would say that anyway?)
You LOVE . . .
big X
LOVE IS . . .
way too hard to define
then something unintelligible
like a person trying to make a new language
xzytttro3lomttyy###
all in blue ink and sent to
whom?

Tiny Bites Life

"I like tiny bites apple, not big apple."
—Connor James, age 2

Everyone is tired.

The grown-ups have watched too much news,

the bus drivers circled the blocks a thousand times.

A little boy throws his cars back into the bucket.

Make it small for us again, oh world. Tiny bites egg,

tiny white cards to paint on with a tiny brush.

A few free minutes.

One blue and silver earring on the sidewalk

    in front of our gate.

Here, let's hang it from the fence, come and get it.

But no one ever will. The blue will fade, the vine twine

    around it.

Maybe the lady with the other single earring

    will preserve it for years.

Make tiny blossoms, Maria Cristina miniature roses

with a giant fragrance, Star of Bethlehem flowers

    popping after rain,

pointed pink and white heads on skinny stalks.

growing in my neighbor's yard but not mine.

Make me always satisfied.

College Town

Blue ibuprofen
scattered across pavement
pain constellation

Read All about It!

Do you miss the newspapers fluttering in the wind?
They used to be everywhere. Now the delivery car
   speeds down
our street, no one subscribes. A city as big as Pittsburgh
has no fresh daily news, in print anyway, it's not right.
   I don't like
all these headlines just drifting in air. I miss
   my journalist father's
attention to grammar, scissors next to newspapers
   on the table,
If you see improper grammar or misspellings, put them
   in this shoebox. I'll take those
clips to work. Everyone had plenty of newspapers
   to start fires
in fireplaces, spread under watercolor projects,
set muddy boots on. Now we wander in a telephonic
transmitted universe. Here are real headlines
   saved from the trash:

RHINO BITE HALTS PETTING PROGRAM

EX-BOYFRIEND GETS FOUR YEARS IN HAIRCUT ASSAULT

DO NOT CONFUSE PEOPLE WITH SCENERY

FARMER EATEN BY OWN HOGS

9-YEAR-OLD LED A PIRATE'S LIFE

HUSBAND HOLDS WIFE'S TEENAGE DIARY HOSTAGE

JUDGE WHO CONSULTED WITH IMAGINARY DWARF SEEKS JOB

INTERNET BLACKOUT TRACED TO BEAVER

CALIFORNIA TRIBE TO APOLOGIZE TO SALMON IN NEW ZEALAND

READER HAS INTERVIEW WITH BABOON

MONKEY CAGED AFTER BITING BANKER

IN STUDY, WOMEN LIKE HEALTHIER BABIES

Owner of 136 Snakes Surrenders Them, Texas

The man had no lights, running water, or air-conditioning

in his home. But he had rats and mice in small boxes

   and cages

to feed his snakes and some of the rodents were sneezing.

His neighbors weren't sure what was going on in there

but heard the miniature sneezes (seriously),

detected a stinky smell,

and worried he was hoarding trash.

Someone called authorities to report

the mystery. They used the word "mistreatment"

but weren't sure of what. Here is a fact:

There is no limit to the number of snakes

a person can own in San Antonio as long as

they have satisfactory living conditions.

Like ventilation, enough water,

toys and games, plenty of exercise room.

If your snake is longer than three feet,

it must live in a cage. I would certainly

hope so.

Folded Cardboard in the Street

is not the box it was born to be.

I worry about cardboard, used so briefly

then pitched or piled near massive bins,

whole congregations of cardboard growing,

this won't work very long

in the world we're in. O lazybones Americans,

the waste feels overwhelming,

unless the cardboard's headed to recycling.

But this is nothing, nothing, nothing,

next to, say, the city of Aleppo,

one of the most gracious metropolises

ever made, over centuries, the arches,

the carefully inlaid tiles,

curling avenues through old markets,

elegant textiles strung on lines for display,

gorgeous curlicued rugs,

what it used to be, what it became.

War is the worst waste—no imagination.

What did anyone gain?

Stumble Leaf

A slow day cracks in half when
a hundred-year-old pecan tree
splits and falls, minutes after we passed.

Hearing sirens, we walk back to check.
Massive half-of-tree crashed across whole street
where I just pushed the baby's stroller.
Who knew? Emergency workers
chop it up with screaming saws,
pitch it into trucks like trash,
cart away a proud monument.

Trees are ferocious.
They might be planning things.
How can we ever again sit calmly in the shade?

Welcome to Hong Kong

1

Steady rain, but walking at 5 a.m.

still feels good—

under my hotel's giant black umbrella

I wander sleeping streets to find

one drenched red carnation

draped across sidewalk

take home to my room

stick it in a glass of water where

it perks up and smiles for 5 whole days

2

Later in sunshine

outside the same flower shop

blossoms swept into neat mounds

I want to ransack the piles

3

Hand-painted black English letters on the wall of a
  blue house
PLEASE DO NOT TAKE OUR FLOWERPOT SECRETLY
but there is no flowerpot anywhere around
so I guess someone did
The "secretly" seems odd
Wonder what was in it
Wonder where it went

4

At school the Lost and Found table
jammed with pencil boxes
kitty cats, princesses, dinosaurs, Batman
outside near a school bus
one brown pencil box in the gutter
crushed by a wheel

5

To hotel doorman standing with hands folded
Sir, can you help me get a taxi?
No, I cannot

6

In the lobby my phone brings
bad news
faraway friend Bryan has died
Could you instantly send something
for us to read at his funeral?
He noticed the world
wandering with appetite
savoring details   quirky Texas
come alive through tiniest towns
back roads he described
Did he ever come to Hong Kong?
He would have loved it
He might have bought the same
polka-dotted washcloth in a sidewalk stall
He would surely have picked up that carnation
We are changed forever
A writer paying attention
underscoring our own lives
passing everything on

Three Wet Report Cards on Camden Street

Sorry, all that homework
and now even your own name
has washed away

Report cards from the late 1970s
dumped in a clump
smudgy grades
Teacher Comment areas bare

Was someone moving and
they fell out of a box?
I'm tempted to leave them
lying by the curb behind
the Catholic school

feeling great sadness

for the hard work of teachers

filling in so many little boxes

dreary evaluating and judging

when what teachers love best

is that spark of discovery

that great question

the shy person

finally speaking from the stage

McD
on
ald's

now breaks up

its own name

on side of cup

attempting sophistication

Years ago in St. Louis, Missouri,

my mom and daddy took me to see

what they said was the second or third

McDonald's in the whole world

It was a novelty

They liked the yellow arches

My daddy said

I think this restaurant is going places

What do you mean? I asked

There will be a lot of them someday

Really? A big sign said they had sold

2 million burgers already

He said there was a Hamburger University in Illinois

recently started by McDonald's people

(whose real name was Kroc)

where you could get a hamburgerology degree

The place didn't seem special to me

I didn't eat hamburgers

didn't like french fries in small sacks

I was a young healthy foods cosmonaut

my dad munching on a crisp potato

mom who usually banned sugar

sipping noisily on vanilla triple-thick shake

I watched a single white paper bag blowing

   onto the highway

from the parking lot

and contemplated the new no-litter laws

that said people who threw trash on the ground

might have to pay a fine

Police! Police!

Years later upon arrival in Tokyo

my host would try to take me

to McDonald's for lunch

Rudely I said No!

and hulked grumpily

down the block by myself

to a local noodle shop

Today there are more than

36,000 McDonald's

in the world

and how many bags have blown

across how many highways?

How many empty cups

dumped by the road?

I've found 37,000 abandoned

mustard packets

all by myself

Guadalupe Street Trash

purple underpants

crushed like a blossom

under Stop sign

we don't want to know

what could cause someone

to lose undergarments

out in public like that

let's say they fell from a laundry basket

I'm carrying purple candles

mountain laurel fragrance

from the Root Candle Company

almost want to light one right here

Take care of yourselves

your clothes

your souls

boys and girls of the world

ROUTE 3
Odds & Ends

Current Events

What have we learned?
There are more crimes
people and governments
            could commit
    than we ever dreamed of

The President We Did Not Vote For

keeps doing things we do not like.

Why are we surprised?

The president we did not vote for

talks uglier than the bully in grade school

who actually did not talk much,

but tripped and punched.

A critic wrote, "He expels the words out of his mouth

like evicted tenants."

The president we did not vote for

does not feel like a president at all

which is why we keep staring at

the two-year-old who did not vote

for anyone, to see what captures his interest.

If you show him a shark

he says *No See That!* which is how I feel about

the president I did not vote for.

The two-year-old loves a book called *Egg*,

perhaps the most perfect book ever made.

Simple, strong, it does not contain a single

extra note. The two-year-old

loves black paint in the paint box most,

it is bravest on the page.

He loves a green crayon but does not like

the point worn down. If he drops half a cracker,

he picks it up and throws it in the trash

which suggests he will grow up to be a noble person.

I remember being told when I was somewhat older

    than two

that growing up is full of trouble and disappointment and

how we deal with it makes us who we are

and right now that is certainly true.

Looking at Any Map

Preferably an old-fashioned crackly
blue/green paper map with seams and folds
spread flat on the table in front of you
not a telephone or GPS map
you feel the myriad ways you might go
like veins inside your body, well-lit
electrical switchboard of breathing and being
and it is stunning how the blood flows.
Follow a river with your finger,
gleam around corners you never
turned yet . . . that back road that seems
to curl into itself and disappear.
There is no disarray in this endless dream of
where we might find ourselves,

no dark fretting, no fear of being late.

No receipts clogging the roses

in the median, no scattered menus

or pizza promotions.

Just pastures between things,

where an Amish buggy

might appear, glowing yellow lantern at dusk,

above the driver's seat,

or groves of lost red maples

glistening near Vanderpool—

a meadow, a mountain, a stream.

Crushed Cup

in the street
in front of our house
seems a hundred years old
but it wasn't here
when I went to bed last night

How does something
become old so quickly?

Refreshing ourselves
means sleeping well
thinking better thoughts
drinking from
a different kind of cup
lifting morning to our lips
that slim pink strip of light
so quickly merging yellow
saying this tastes like
a hopeful note
brave beverage
something better
we could be together

Not a Bagel, But . . .

A cup lid rolled away
in a strong wind
like a happy wheel
gone free,
careened
down the street
without falling over
like in David Ignatow's
wondrous poem "The Bagel"
from my high school textbook.
David dropped his bagel
and it rolled. While chasing after it
he entered the moment
so thoroughly
he became a bagel too
at least in metaphor
feeling "strangely happy with"
himself.
This helped me in high school.
Despite high school, we might still be happy.
I did not become a plastic cup lid
but felt so happy for
an image from a poem which can
stay with you your whole life.

Barbara

My friend with a hundred handbags
   a thousand bracelets
   and the best taste of
      any person I know
also collects
   rusted metal scraps
she finds under her tires
     in the coffee shop parking lot
a hinge
   a bracket
     a clamp
      a key
Rust carries the true beauty of time
   She saves the scraps
     in a basket
      in a drawer
We were standing outside
   saying good-bye
     and her eye caught
a glint in the gutter
   a twist
     of light

Mysteries of Humankind

One rotten white sock
at Alma's front gate—
    we need to talk to Alma.

Who throws away water bottles
    still full?
    Insult to water.

Three people on one block insulted water.

Trash likes to congregate at fences—
must be their convention site.

Rubber heel of a black shoe—say, wanderer,
you felt crooked the rest of the day, I'll bet.

People eat half a stick of venison jerky,
then pitch the rest by the fire hydrant,
still in wrapper.
            Poor deer.

We Make Our Own Trash

*"I just threw all the notes on my desk away without looking at them.
Now I never have to do anything, ever again."*

—*John Lurie*

Plans and intentions

    way a brain works

hip hop   easy to do something *in the future*

    That's a good idea!

            Why not?

Pitch that worry into the dumpster please!

      Say no say no say no

        When some of us

    were growing up   you could only post

with tape or thumbtack   no convenient sticky pages

      no digital archives

forehead of days covered   with thumbtacks

hard to see anything much

      through flapping scraps

Famous People

1

O. Henry lived in our neighborhood
and wrote stories here
before he went to jail for tax evasion
or embezzlement
whatever he did or didn't do
His pen name is engraved
in the sidewalk
on South Presa Street
with an arrow pointing to
where he used to live
William Sydney Porter
was his real name
His cottage was moved
to rest over by the jail
so his ghost might feel more at home
There's a community garden now
in his old hood
filled with tiny bourbon bottles
rosemary bushes gone to seed
near where his writing table used to be
a block replete with trash

He liked plot twists at the ends
of his stories
How would he twist this?
Maybe the people who upgrade their energies
at the super health juice factory
go wild after they drink so much celery and carrot
they clean out the backseats and trunks
of their cars right there
throwing it all on the ground
atop O. Henry's name
right over posterity
as if a cloud passed over the moon

2

Rudolf Staffel the great ceramicist
grew up on Cedar Street
He built a kiln in his backyard
hiked with young artist friends to
the small Alsatian town of Castroville
twenty-three miles from San Antonio
tiny and picturesque
to paint for the weekend
then walked home
Bet they didn't see much trash

Or if they did, they buried it
Those dedicated young artists

I think Rudi would have liked to know
the ink-maker forager named Jason Logan
who hikes around Central Park
and river valleys to collect
foliage and rubbish
making gorgeous ink from
sumac, pokeweeds, tobacco, iron scraps
boiling acorns with pennies
or goldenrod

Sometimes I just ask myself
Where have we gone wrong?
Why don't we all know
how to make things from scratch?
Why can't I build a kiln
or make ink?

Then again
as a beloved older artist
Rudolf hated doing laundry
so visited Goodwill repeatedly to buy

stacks of shirts

flannel, cotton, linen, checkered

whole towers of folded shirts

he kept by his bed

After wearing the shirts

he gave them back to Goodwill

Trash Talk 326

Did anyone ever say you were their girlfriend
or boyfriend and you barely even knew them?

Did they tell your friends they had insight
and could guess what you might do next?

Did they say you called them when you
didn't even know their number?

What did you do about people like this?
Did you argue, tell them off?

Or walk calmly past them in the hallway
as if they were a locker or a clock?

They Are Thinking about Giving Tickets

In Hamtramck by Detroit,
　　once called a super-hip neighborhood
　　　　by the *Utne Reader* magazine,
　　the litter keeps piling up.
Stop! said the Polish people, the Germans, the Yemeni
　families,
　　　　Bangladeshis, Bosnians, we have enough
　troubles
　　where we came from, can't you tidy
after yourselves?
They would rather focus on bakeries and festivals,
　　rich tapestries of languages, fragrant phyllo
　pastries,
　　　　the multiculti flow,
　　than sandwich wrappers blowing in the wind.
Scrappy lots brimming with trash—some people suggest
　giving tickets, fines attached, like traffic tickets,
　　to anyone with litter near their home
　　　Sir, do you live here?
I know it would be problematic.
　　　　You could blame wind or your neighbors.
Or, you could bow to the task.

Tony's Trash

When my friend Tony was very sick
he worried about his small apartment
   high over the river
Who would empty it when he died?
He gave me a key
told me to pass on his two carpets
       he called magic flying carpets
  to my mom
We were the last people to see him
    except for a nurse
He fluttered his fingers at us
He really believed in heaven

I arrived after his death
    to find his apartment stripped bare
  door standing wide open
all his clothes and big shoes gone
his little table and chairs and plants
  even his walker
His neighbors had been hard at work
I had to track down those carpets
but in the trash can five giant crystal teardrops

on a long thread

that had hung in his window

the prettiest thing he owned

thrown away

I could imagine him watching rainbow light shimmer

through refracting teardrops

as he wrote his one million emails to the

city council the mayor the police chief

about all the injustice in the city he wanted to heal

It pained him personally to see a dirty drunken man

sleeping by flowerpots on the corner

or anxious human beings lined up

clutching paperwork outside

the Mexican consulate on the other corner

Why didn't we take better care of one another?

Noise too loud outside the cathedral

Trash bins overflowing

Tony! Tony! None of us are perfect!

He believed in angels though

He was the old world town crier riveted by wrong

unseen rainbow tears flowing down his walls

Ilse's Trash

In the year 1999, our ninety-nine-year-old neighbor died—
such a disappointment. We'd been planning
a big party on her porch for one hundred.
I couldn't attend the estate sale of her belongings
because I loved her too much. But I would carry
donation boxes to the Conservation Society.
Loading my trunk, I peered sideways to see
vintage school magazines *Huisache* from 1916—
peeking from the trash. I plucked and kept them.

Reading them later I felt heartbroken to have missed
the chance to get "a dandy drink at Nester's Fountain."
No one had ever suggested that my own generation
might "whoop things up with a lot more vim" if we
only wore the right clothes. Had the boys in my life
contemplated the "long step from knickerbockers to
trousers" the way boys of Ilse's class had?
But here's the kicker.
An article called "Art Department" begins,
"There was a time when people . . . thought that art
was a subject too far removed from everyday life
to be taught with the other subjects of the classroom.

At present we are coming to realize that art is
involved in the life of each and every person. . . . "

Obvious Necessity of Art—in 1916!!
(Also the writer wondered why a new art program
offered in high school had eighty students signed up,
only five of whom were boys. He said it was
obvious the "fairer sex" was more cultivated
and would save us all with beauty and vision.)
Dear Boards of Education trimming curriculums,
attention please! Honor your history!
Dear Ilse, queen of our neighborhood forever,
restore us to an artful life
that kept you smiling so long.

Junk Mail

The great poet
William Stanley Merwin
known as W. S.
wrote first drafts of his poems
on junk mail envelopes
plucked from the garbage
so he never had to worry
about wasting paper
or being perfect

Prince Charles Please

Prince Charles has been worrying about plastic waste

for forty years but doesn't want to say "I told you so."

Why not? Please do!

Someone needs to.

Donald Trump says nearly every sentence

three times, as if he's trying to find, or remember it.

I heard this terrible thing,

this really really very terrible thing,

this truly terrible thing—

soon there will be more plastic in the oceans than fish.

Hordes of strange colors

knotted in seaweed, bobbing in waves.

Sheikhs, prime ministers, princes,

please take your podiums, platforms, promises

straight to the trash dumps where they belong!

Trash Talk 1

You are not a worthy person
You were born in a shroud of sins.
Come to me, believe what I believe,
And you will be healed.

ROUTE 4
Willy-nilly

Things I Found Today

Numerous cigar wrappers. Large font warning:
Cigars are not better for your health
than cigarettes. (I would hardly think so.
Much bigger, to begin with . . .)

Little plastic white hanger from a child's dress.

Tags.

A rice box.

Two dill pickles still in brine in their jar.

Two spools of green wire.

An entire breakfast on the bridge—scrambled eggs,
     meat, biscuit—
in a plastic box.

Too many half-drunk sodas.

One smashed glass mug in front of

    the nicest person's house.

Bits and pieces, snips and sneezes.

A headless squirrel I did not pick up.

RACCOON AT WORK.

Straws & spoons & a Styrofoam cup

in three pieces.

One treasure:

blue baby mitten with polka dots,

the word HEROES knitted in.

Attention

A man named his baby daughter
because of a playing card he found on the ground.
No one can remember the details
and neither of his daughters are named
Queen or Ace
but we remember the location of the
playing card, near Alamo Music Company,
under the sign
that says *Music heals,*
See the Music Doctor,
and how, at one moment,
he was looking down.

In high school, a woman in my dream told me
to give a message to a blind girl in my class—
I'm her mother,
tell her not to kill herself.
My thought upon awakening—
Why doesn't she tell her directly?
I believed in dreams but
felt crazy chasing a girl I barely knew down a hall,
then stuttering such words.

Later the girl thanked me
saying the message meant more
since it came through someone else.
"It was true. My mother is dead.
And that is what I was going to do."

Strange Things Keep Happening: Houston

A concierge crosses the gleaming hotel lobby
to hand me a single silver paper clip.
Excuse me, did you lose this?
I don't believe so.
Nevertheless I take it,
pop it into my pocket,
staring at him in wonder.
Out of all the people
milling around this lobby
munching cupcakes,
how on earth
did he determine
I am a person
who would have considered
picking it up?

New Year

Where is the spine of a year?
A year begins all curled up
blank on a page. Not even a single day
has stretched its arms out yet.
It could do anything.

The first stranger I see
at a corner downtown
marked by concrete trash bins
empty for once
wears a black sweatshirt
with large white letters:
ALL I CARE ABOUT IS HUNTING
AND MAYBE LIKE 3 PEOPLE
AND BEER.
All year I can say to myself
He is not my father.
I am not his daughter.

Bits

Consider the loneliness of trash
pummeled, blown, unloved
Let's visit the trash
after the rain
See if it feels better

Some things too grim to touch
potato chip bag
filled with vomit
under innocent cactus

Twigs are not trash
though sometimes they clutter
fallen willy-nilly
after big rains
You have to sweep them
or your thoughts
feel scattered too

Deep inside tall daisies

snippet of white wrapper

hiding away

impersonating a blossom

Secret troves of trash

Glass bottles tucked between

two brick buildings on South Alamo

Is this their clubhouse?

little cave hideaway

orange juice boxes ganging up

causing trouble

On South Flores

a woman with grocery cart

piled sky-high

black trash sacks of clinking cans

I know where she's going

blocks away in morning gray

to sell the cans

before the heat strikes

We used to sell our pecans there too

or have them cracked

so we could shell them more easily

Now there aren't as many pecans

Trees are tired

Trees are falling over onto the street

People are tired

Her tipsy cart has a wavering wheel

Cigarette butts

pepper the pavement

some people didn't get the news yet

or didn't believe it

maybe they're already dead

and those butts are fossilized

something elegant about a cigarette box though

hate to say it but even lying in the street

that shiny silver lining seems appealing

neat flappable lid

perhaps part of addiction

plants can't be trash

     buds   nuts   yellow pollen curlicues

Buddhist abandon

  let go   *let go*   *let go*

Why don't we find more toys?

Stuffed animals

toppled out of strollers?

Metal cars & fire trucks

with spinny wheels

Maybe this is the one thing

everyone picks up

roar of trash truck lumbering down the street

   weirdly exhilarating

now we get back to

          beginning again

Taxpayer Money

When I was growing up I never thought about

taxpayer money because I was not a taxpayer

    pockets of regret   human destiny

        nagging feelings

I don't want to be paying for weapons

used in other countries against innocent people

    incomplete wishes

        withheld sentences

unspoken best thoughts

      scattered minutes

Is regret its own kind of trash?

      Maybe it helps us move forward

    be better

my neighbor resents paying the fee for trash collection

    on our utilities bills

In my opinion   it could never be enough

Trash Talk 7,299

My fingers shiver

when I'm out without my gear

Some scrap calls to me

juice box

looking ill at ease

among purple grasses

It's so hard just to walk by

as if I don't see it

yeah yeah yeah

stepping over

leaving it be

Trash Walk 1,021

Never alone

Beneath our feet

Lost neighborhoods echoing

Three Blank Index Cards

1

dropped outside architecture office

stand-up desks   cool silver lamps

hey architects!

let's hear it for tiny houses!

2

Were these for someone's

grocery list? Their next boring meeting

with developers?

Blank is delicious

Blank could be anything

A little girl named Harriet left messages

scrawled on index cards

under herb pots on her neighbors' stoops

You are not alone

or

Free joy in the sky

Look up!

What Makes People the Way They Are?

I finished my pineapple juice
       and will now throw the can down
by the road

I am rich
but I need more
       more

          more

Someone else
     does cleanup

YOU ARE HERE

scrawled in cement
on St. Mary's near Madison Street
I have walked this sidewalk
so many times
missing that message
and only today
picking up pill bottles
and tissue
from a side-of-the-road
infirmary
I guess
I really was
here

Happy Day

News flash: finally the long-vacant Hedrick Building
is turning into apartments and a hotel!
It's so exciting to see the ugly 1960s "aluminum
    cladding"
removed from the gorgeous "terra-cotta Spanish colonial
    detailing."
We always knew something beautiful was under there
and guess what else?! Seventeen truckloads of
    pigeon droppings
were carted away from the roof and windowsills
Seventeen truckloads! It's like a Tom Waits song.
Can we even imagine how sleek that building must feel?

Back Streets of Ledbury, Herefordshire, England

Raining in gray twilight

I wandered boots & slicker

far from home

thinking of John Masefield the great poet

who grew up in Ledbury writing poems

about going down to the sea though he

supposedly feared water

and Elizabeth Barrett the great poet

"Let me count the ways" she loved

Robert Browning another great poet

though her daddy wouldn't talk to her

after she married him

Let us count the ways daddies can be nice or mean

Let us count the mysteries   ripples of sound

in a quiet evening in a quiet town

Ledbury Letterpress founded in 1875

my new oasis

Martin the master printer

approved my pawing through his rubbish

sheaves of succulent margins in the bins—

long thin creamy strips of paper

delicious as frosted cakes

stacks and heaps of layers

perfect for poem writing

in any era of history

Evening rolled in

The print shop locked its doors

nothing more haunting than

drifting invisibility

Maybe it's the closest we come to being

omniscient

floating past a row of mailboxes

none of them mine

finding on the ground

a thick red balloon with all its breath gone out

on a blue stick

confetti springing from the stick

looks like it was shot out of a cannon

so exhausted

the party's over!

stick it in my pocket   ask kids at school

the next day   what kind of balloon is this?

They say they have never seen such a thing

at any party in their town   maybe it's for babies

we're at John Masefield High School

they know more about him

than kids in Paterson, New Jersey

know about William Carlos Williams

They're nice to me   volunteering to read their poems

cocoons of syllables knitted into the air

I love them though I will walk out of this school

and never see it again

Pop!

let us count

the new poems

we could write

Why Are We So Messy?

Tinfoil from breakfast taco
shredded into fringes now
shiny ringlets

Pounded paper cups a thud
rustle of wistfulness
Why are we so lazy
Why are we so listless
All the joggers and dog walkers
bicycles parked at bicycle stands
electric scooters now abandoned all over town
Relentless relaxation
but pitch the blue bubblegum wrapper
into the ditch

Litter
tastes
bitter.

I mean,
if you ate it,

it would.

People picking dinner

out of cans.

I close my eyes.

This is different.

This is super

hard times.

Arriving in Mumbai

still called Bombay by everyone c'mon people

taxi lights picking out

heaps   hillocks   mountains

of trash   I'd been to India so many times

but never these back streets before dawn

such a contrast to

swept shrines

blossoming parks

succulent beaches

rich museums

even a toilet museum honoring sanitation

Being a trash collector definitely changes

how you look at the world

What will happen to us?

ROUTE 5

Residue

Trash Talk 948

Maricela asks an audience,

What are you doing to show resistance?

It is her farewell to the crowd.

We clap loudly,

step into the dark.

My friend Phil tells me someone is

misinterpreting my poem "Jerusalem"

in an article, saying it advocates violence.

Ho hum. What a dumb reader.

I never Google myself to find out what anyone says—

such a way to go crazy that might be.

But all night I toss and turn.

Have you ever been insulted?

Has anyone misinterpreted what you said?

Have you tossed and turned?

What are we doing to show resistance?

To clear my thoughts next morning,

I go pick up more trash at the Number 11B bus stop.

Reese's Peanut Butter Cup wrappers,

haven't seen these in a long time.

Empty blue matchbox. A lost wheel,

the kind an office chair might miss,

a red comb with a long handle,

broken headlight from a bike,

three straws, four jelly containers,

two pennies, orange peelings,

unwrapped food scraps are always a different story,

you leave them to return to earth,

and then I find a giant eagle feather

and my brain settles down.

Movies

The only great movie star I ever knew personally
flipped when I discarded a baggie in her kitchen.
She snatched it from the trash,
What are you thinking? We KEEP these! We REUSE them!
rinsed it thoroughly, clipped it to a small sculpture
   of hooks
to dry. I felt ashamed. Tried to be a better person
   the rest of the
evening, *I recycle everything too,* but realized I don't,
if throwing out a baggie was automatic.
I ate every crumb from my plate.
Washed the dishes by hand so carefully.
She said she would use a baggie for a whole year
until it tore.

I don't have many famous friends anymore,
which makes me think surely I did many other bad
annoying things and deserve to be picking up trash
with a tongs for the rest of my days. I still love the movies,
though. Sometimes when the lights switch on after a movie
and we hike the aisle stretching our stiff legs,
teetering a little, it's almost more than I can bear

to pass all those empty popcorn tubs and massive

    soda cups

scattered stickily between rows. I want to help the ushers

tidy the joint before the late show, I want to hold

the movie in my heart and bend down and use

a little whisk broom and dustpan like stylists

once favored in shop windows of department stores

to make everything look glamorous again.

Vero Beach Revival

Sleeping in Florida

waves just down the block

you feel more like a wave yourself

It's a redemption

Coming and going of language

Talking to a man whose grandpa

paved the road that is now the big road

People still go way back

Scattered gray shells spelling a message

not a scrap of trash on a long gray beach

Shells belong here   A   B   C

You're just visiting

Seven hundred acres where cattle graze

I never think of cattle in Florida

Meeting someone you met a long time ago

by another beach

Memory its own scattering of shells

Perfect turquoise/white guesthouse

holding jugs of local orange juice

bowls of local grapefruits

pink and purple tulips

Every Florida memory you ever had

skitters across the sky

No See That

It's what little Connor says for buffaloes or dinosaurs
or the friendly lion on *Daniel Tiger's Neighborhood*.
Daniel seems more like a boy than a tiger.
The lion pops from a forest wearing his large mane
and Connor turns away.

When do we turn?

We turn away from Breaking News,
pick everything up by osmosis,
then can't stop watching it.
All sucked in, like crumbs vacuumed off a rug.
We want to love Puerto Rico from the bottom up.
Tell Palestine and Syria we wish to help them.
Spread the word.

Some days my goal is not to annoy anyone.
No see that daddy slap his girl when she can't
make up her mind. No see mean and selfish,
desperation to be noticed, bigger, better,
nokay, no-how, let's try a gentler,
spacious way to be. The fluffy cat
afraid of babies
sleeps on his back for hours
while rain pours outside.
He snores so quietly the room feels cleansed.
Rhythm rising from the roots.

Down in the dirt after dark,
one frog
singing.

Trash Mottoes

Tend to your own refuse, yes.

Expect someone else to bend, no.

Wipe the counter clean, please.

If you pitch your rubbish into a rosebush,

the roses will notice it.

Things usually do not just fall—out of baskets, cars.

Usually we drop them. We carry too much.

Why do we need so much?

Waiting is not an excuse for littering.

People apparently lose their good character

    at airport gates.

Pizza boxes! Napkins! Coffee cups! Junky junky!

Is this okay because you're only here for forty minutes?

Yes, it's okay to pile paper mail on your compost.

Envelopes will disappear more slowly than peelings

but soon blend in.

For a while we raised worms in a giant green canister.

We fed them our compost, they ate it overnight.

They were fat and luscious, happy worms,

then we released them into the soil like

    little garbage trucks

and our plants seemed happier too. It's time to

    raise worms

and learn how to weave again. My friend Pecos

meditated on a single poem while he wove

    a thick blue shawl.

Even looking at the photos of his patient progress

makes me feel warm.

All we have, all we do with it . . .

Trash Walk 1331

If possible
check out trash cans in art rooms.
Palettes are glorious.

Stephen Foster

Once my dad and I hiked to an abandoned
   crumbling hotel
deep in a Florida forest where the composer
Stephen Foster had once stayed.
We tiptoed through sagging wooden doors to the lobby
to find receipts—receipts!—from fifty years before
scattered across the floor.
Names of guests elegantly scrawled by hand.
The yellowed papers seemed holy, we could touch
but could not take them. I hoped for pillows, coverlets,
teapots, just to see the past spread haunted before us,
but people had been ransacking that place for years. There
were trash cans—old round wire cans poked in on
   one side,
and a rotten enamel sink. A notebook's spine,
we had stepped out of time.
My father muttered, *Where are all these people now?*
He smiled. He seemed relieved.
The thought of them dead did not depress him.
He said what he always said, everywhere we ever went,
I wonder what this place would cost.
Then a Stephen Foster tune—*humm humm humm*—
   burst from my mouth loudly,
and echoed. As if I had just checked in.

Central School

Ferguson, Missouri, is also a peaceful place
filled with vintage houses, creeks and grass,
an old train rattling on the overpass,
or is the train station an ice cream shoppe now?
It might be an ice cream shoppe.
And I grew up there.
One tree planted by my German grandpa now cut down,
now chunky stump,
but its twin tree is enormous.
Wabash Lake, ducks, loving library, local restaurants,
once too white, now black and white mixed,
streets with the same names,
organic farm still prospering, I found the crack
in a sidewalk I used to trip on.
Playground. Auto parts. Mary Moore's house
still brown, by the school where we dreamed our dreams
and did our mischief. Shockingly even the baseball field
    backstop
is the same and it seemed old back then. But here's my
    holiest moment:
After I was grown, on a trip home in summer heat,

the school janitor let me into my old second grade

    classroom.

"Don't tell anyone I haven't dumped all the trash yet!"

On top of the can right there, a hand-lettered dictionary,

flipped open to the *L* page, and every

    most important word

of life lined up handwritten—*Love, Learn, Lose, Laugh*—

and thrown away. How could anyone

throw that away? A neat little dictionary—

I took it. Thought about second grade being the

best grade, how the world opened wide in second grade,

and we stood in dignity reciting poems to one another,

Loving Language, and our teacher Mrs. Lane told us,

Don't worry if you make a mistake. We had Smile Day.

She was firm but kind. How far we travel

to find first things still shining, embedded gems,

Luminous Lessons of every age. We learned

a song called "Look for the Silver Lining"

and we sang it from the stage.

Nothing

Nothing a child
ever does
is trash.
It is
practice.

Connor James, Age 3 (spoken poems)

My bus was going by
and it didn't even look at me.
It just left me here.

Be nice to my dada!
Be nice to my dada!
If you are not nice to my dada,
you should not have a mouth.

Not My Problem

Izzy grins, "I have my own problems"
when you start telling him yours.

Problems as pivots. Something had to turn
or move for them to dissolve.

You can't help thinking about trash
during hurricanes, floods, earthquakes.

Where does it all go?
How much more is born?

Wet trash is heavier than dry trash.
If a whole city gets devastated, what happens next?

Baghdad! Houston! San Juan! It's everyone's problem.
Don't pretend you're exempt
just because you have a big trash can and a maid.
Ha ha just kidding about the maid.
In hotel rooms I clean up for the housekeeper
before she comes.

Trash tells its story. Who you are,
how you spend your days.

The Potato

The potato that slept
in Idaho soil
kept its eyes closed while dreaming.
It only opened them a crack
when dug up, loaded onto a truck.
It wondered where it might go,
potatoes popular in almost
every world cuisine, but
landed in a nearby factory
with a million comrades where
it was peeled and sliced,
then packaged in a giant plastic bag.
In darkness it traveled

to a very cold room

in a mysterious place filled with

sizzling grease and metal baskets

and lived there a while.

No reason now to open its eyes.

Like a bad dream, it was

lowered into the heat, then

plopped into a small cardboard envelope

which turned up today

on Labor Street,

two French fries languishing

in corpse-like abandon.

Not even a bird would eat them.

Penny

Penny on the Salt Lake City
airport floor, right after I thought of you
so hard. How long
have you been gone?
You will never be gone.
It was shining in the gate of
little planes to smaller places,
Sun Valley, Casper.
Picking up the light.
As those towns do.
As you would have loved to see.

Lately the Moon

has been quite demanding.
Come out and look at me!
She seems swollen.
Her radiance blooms
through the trees.

The internet was invented,
then we could all live
in our own little worlds.
Or try to inhabit one another's—
there were ways to live
vicariously—
as if that other person's struggle
were yours too,
or that musician was singing
in your room.
Extroverts and introverts both
went underground
but felt more connected because
they kept throwing their comments around.
You could look up anything now.
Leaving Amish Paradise!
A Hermit Lives in a Cave!
So much to like, so much to be wary of.

People finding one another across the miles.

And plenty of trash scattered across the air.

You could disappear in there,

get lost so easily,

hours compressing into clicks.

On the other hand

you could go back to the street

glistening in that bright moonlight,

back to the cooling pavement,

and pick up sticks.

Ideas for Writing, Recycling, Reclaiming

1. Picking up trash is not depressing, since you are doing something positive. A solitary trash walk will offer an instant boost of positivism—your dopamine level instantly rises. (A scientific fact I just made up, but I do think it's true.) You see results right in front of you, which is pleasant for the instant-gratification part of your psyche. Picking up trash by yourself is not messy, yucky, or creepy. If you carry a nice fresh bag (I do feel a little guilty about the bag and sometimes use a recyclable paper grocery bag), wear protective gloves, and carry tongs, it is simply cleansing—refreshing in the extreme. People speak to you with gratitude. But also you are slightly invisible, which is its own pleasure.

2. Write about what you find. You learn a lot about human nature while doing this. Why do people throw certain things away? What do these leavings tell you about your neighbors? Imagine the litterer. Create a character study from everything you find on one day, as if it all came from one person. Or write a story including 5–10 of the items you find.

3. Picking up trash with someone else is a pleasantly social, somehow humorous activity. You never run out of conversational material. Together, you can look back at the blocks behind you with a feeling of pride—deeper investment in your community's shared ground. It's relaxing. You're doing something useful and heartening, flexing your body.

4. Have a trash-pickup birthday party. The "games" can be . . . making art out of found objects. Did you know that the New York and San Francisco sanitation departments have had

artist-in-residence programs for quite a while now? Be an artist, yourself, with some of what you find. The party favors? No telling. Recently I found eight perfect unopened deodorant sticks in a plant container by a bridge. And a green bath rug. I didn't take any of this home. But a super-bouncy pink-and-white ball, discovered lodged in a bush, went home from New York City with me.

5. Earth Day surely hosts countless trash awareness activities already. Why not have Earth Day every Saturday or Sunday? An hour of cleansing—for the domain you select, as for the mind. Select a single block to tend. Be the caretaker of four blocks near your home. If you live near a beach, adopt a section of sand. Focus on a single area and really get to know it.

6. Be a trash mentor for little kids. Take some younger people on a trash walk with you to trigger their awareness—this could easily change their lives.

7. When a special event is happening, be the trash collector for the neighborhood in question. Recently a gorgeous new modern art museum—RUBY CITY—opened in our San Antonio neighborhood. This museum will share the collection of a late, great artist and arts philanthropist—Linda Pace. The museum will always be free. It was recently named by *Time Magazine* as one of the 100 new magical places in the world. I walk on Camp Street, where Ruby City has been built, very often, en route to the post office. And I know how trash collects by the old San Pedro Creek, along the curbs and under the trees, in the niches of rock leading down to the water. I couldn't stand the thought that so many people would be coming to our 'hood for Grand Opening Day, and might see a mess scattered before them. So starting early that morning, a personal intensive began, and by the time the crowds and mariachis and mayor

arrived, Camp Street was sleek and litter-free. It was a day of glory for everyone who had looked forward to the museum, and a day of secret (till now) glory for the trash collector.

8. Holding ourselves accountable is not a frivolous activity. It might not be a bad idea to post temporary signs in heavily trashed areas reminding people of this, in whatever format you choose.

9. Write a letter to a particular piece of trash.

10. Have you ever found something valuable? I had an elder friend (Tony, he's in this book) who used a walker but nevertheless walked for miles, regularly, and somehow kept finding folded twenty-dollar bills. What have you found that seemed valuable to you? Write about it.

11. With your classmates, save all the trash you collect around your own schoolyard for a whole month. Create a trash "happening"—an exhibition of your bounty, before sending it to the landfill or recycling center. Perhaps share a documentary film on a related trash topic—have a "Town Hall" meeting with your friends, invite parents and community members.

It's never too late to make things better. Understanding them more might help.

Index of First Lines

Ferguson, Missouri, is also a peaceful place 138

has been quite demanding. 146
He wads Kleenex into balls 47

I finished my pineapple juice 115
If possible 136
In a California redwood forest 34
In Hamtramck by Detroit, 90
in the street 80
In the year 1999, our ninety-nine-year-old
     neighbor died—93
is not the box it was born to be. 61
It may seem cruel, but surely for the greater good. 40
It must have lived in the back pocket 42
It says, I do not care 30
It's what little Connor says for buffaloes or dinosaurs 132
Izzy grins, "I have my own problems" 142

keeps doing things we do not like. 76

Let's just throw it away. 15

Maricela asks an audience, 127
My bus was going by 141
My fingers shiver 112
My friend with a hundred handbags 82

Acknowledgments

"Taking Out the Trash" first appeared on Poem-A-Day, The Academy of American Poets website, 2018.

David Sedaris's observation included in the introduction first appeared in a magazine article ("Stepping Out," *The New Yorker*, June 30, 2014).

James Poniewozik wrote the comment included in "The President We Did Not Vote For" ("Trump's Tweets Pivot, Loudly, to Video," *New York Times*, September 12, 2018).

Kevin Henkes wrote the perfect book called *Egg* (Greenwillow Books, 2017).

John Lurie's remark comes from his very appealing Twitter stream.

"World of the future, we thirsted" appeared first in *The New Yorker*, July 29, 2019; p. 56.

Lifetime gratitude to W. S. Merwin, who lives forever in his poems, who guided us so well through his voice of immense compassion.